SEXUAL
Skeletons

Zoë Dee

Zoë Dee

Copyright © 2018. Zoe Dee Speaks. All rights reserved.

Cover Photo by NeONBRAND on <u>Unsplash</u>

Zoë Dee

Dedication

This book is dedicated to the boys and girls inside of women and men that desire freedom. It is too often that society will bombard us with filth, yet when we fall into the temptations of that filth, we are shunned – as if we asked to have the lustful desires of our sinful nature. Because of this, it's hard to break the silence and just admit that we have a problem and that we want help. It's hard to admit that we have desires that we know are unnatural, and we don't know what to do with them. I dedicate this book to those that are afraid to speak out. I want you to know that the desires that you feel, however unnatural – however sinful, there is a way to be free. I am a testament of that freedom. So, I share my story with you, in hopes that 1) you no longer feel alone or ashamed and 2) you know that redemptive power and deliverance does exist. It is by sharing this message that I hope the Holy Spirit's mighty power will breathe on your spirit as you read the words of this book; and where the Spirit of the Lord is, there is liberty. I say – read with an expectation of freedom from the bondage of sexual perversion over your life.

With love and grace,

Zoë

Table of Contents

1. Introduction

2. If These Skeletons Could Talk   6

3. Born in Sin, Shaped in Iniquity   18

4. Consensual   27

Introduction

I didn't think that this part of my story would ever need to be told. Wait. No. I guess in a sense that's not the truth. If I really had to be honest (which obviously is the goal of this book), truth is, I really didn't *want* to tell it. I mean, how *do* you tell it? How do you go before the world and expose the things that are supposed to be silent? How do you expose the things that are never supposed to be talked about? How do you expose the things that are *never* supposed to even be remembered? The past is the past, right? Shouldn't it be left there? *"Time heals all wounds"* right? After all, how could a dark little secret like incest affect anyone else in my life? Most importantly, how do the things, the secrets that you bury remain *alive*?

So why now? Why this moment? I don't know; something about seeing the next generation raised in perversion – in fact, a more perverted society than I was raised and wondering, *"What if they're experiencing the same? Yeah, what if they're kissing and touching each other, or worst, having sex?? What if they're curious enough?"*

If I can be even more honest, I write this book with a little fear. Writing a book that exposes your hurts and past life is one thing, when you're unashamed of it all. But if I can be honest, as I'm trying to be, I would say there's still a little shame here. Why? I don't quite know. But what I do know is that the devil hides in the guilt and shame, and I don't want to leave the devil any room to continue his work.

At the end of the day, I know for sure that I am not a victim of my past; no, I am *a victor* over my past and of my present and future. Yes, this I know. And it sounds so victorious, doesn't it? But why does it still leave me with a, "*Oooooouuuuu, look what you did*," feeling? A feeling that makes me want to run back into the closet; a feeling that makes me want to bury it again, hoping it is something that we never have to talk about.

*Deep breath. *

Unfortunately for us, it is not. We have to talk about it. I apologize. Or rather should I say, "Sorry, not sorry." It is not one of those things we can continue to sweep under the rug. It's not even one of those things that we even joke about. HA! (Sarcastically speaking, or writing should I say.) It becomes *that* deep, and *that* silenced you know?

This is one of those books that will bring you the truth in raw form. It may piss you off or just make you sad. You may even read this not with compassion but with judgement. You may talk about me and say, "*How could they?*" But I should warn you before I continue - be careful of what you judge, for that same judgement you sow *will* return to you, pressed down, shaken together, and running over! Anyway, I'm not sure what your reaction will be.

But the purpose is to tell a recurring story. The script of it is pretty much the same, with only the cast members changing from time to time – and by that, from generation to generation. See, I wasn't given the popular messages to write about, nor the entertaining messages. I wasn't given the, "*God's gone bless ya really good*" messages. The messages I was given, however, are redemptive in nature and they speak to a sexually perverted and dying culture of people – my Father's people, whom He cares deeply for.

This is a call to purity in more ways than one, because we need reformation, we need a revival. We need to understand that our actions do have consequences, and that what we do not only affects us but affects those that are close to us – our children, grandchildren, etc. We need to understand that sex is more than a physical occurrence, but a spiritual one and because of that we must absolutely stop playing with it! Most importantly, we need to understand that we need the fire of the Holy Spirit, the consuming fire, to burn every residue of sexual sin that the enemy has had to permission to exploit in our lives.

Zoë Dee

"If These Bones Could Talk"

A skeleton: A framework of support, founding structure.

I don't know where these sexual skeletons began in my family; and I may never know. So, I'll start with where it began with me. Yet, sadly much of my memory is clouded by the deception of my brain. Would it shock you to know that for much of my life, I have selectively forgotten these things ever existed? That's the deception. The deception that says, *"That didn't happen."* The deception that says, *"It doesn't matter."* The deception that says, *"Close your mouth and don't talk about that, leave the past in the past little girl."* Or the deception that says, *"All lil' kids did that...it's normal."*

If it's so normal, why don't conversations at the family table ever come up like, *"Oh you remember when Lil Mama and NuNu use to kiss each other under the covers."* We are highly deceived, and mainly because we want to be. It's kind of the same as wanting to believe a cheating man isn't cheating, but you know that he is because the evidence is front and center. It's like believing the lies because the truth is too hard to accept.

But I wonder, why doesn't deception speak to my skeletons; I mean, the past is indeed the past and this stuff should be dead and buried – otherwise they wouldn't be skeletons. I obviously didn't realize that skeletons were sustainable without flesh; that they are indeed the major framework or foundation to my entire identity. Did you know that you can identify someone that is dead from their dental records? Well see, that's what these sexual skeletons are doing for me. These skeletons somehow and somewhere keep alive the jagged memories, regardless of how much I want to forget them.

These skeletons: If they could speak back, they would say…

"You remember those days at Grandma's house? Those days where you could walk in, see her bright pie face smile, an array of sunshine bringing light to the many plants sitting in front of it? You remember how it would be you, your siblings, your cousins…? You remember how Grandma use to leave that cigarette butt on the sink, never thinking you'd take a puff but eventually you did, because you were way too curious to let it sit alone? Or what about only having to eat those 'old folks' cereal' because she wasn't going to give you any other options. Yes, you remember. So, you remember that day too. It was a normal day, a pretty regular day - but it only takes a few seconds of a regular day to change your life forever."

My skeletons would remind me that on just a regular day at Grandma's little apartment in my hometown is where incest and bisexual lust entered my life physically. I'm sure I was supposed to have been napping, but I never liked naps; I would rather have been writing or reading. Nevertheless, it began.

The skeletons remind me of how my female cousin and I began to fondle each other, on what I could no longer refer to as a regular day. Clothes on or off, I don't recall. There's that deception again, wanting me to believe that since I can't remember it, then it either didn't happen or it doesn't matter. But see, I do remember the kisses, oddly enough. Yes, I remember us kissing and I remember being under the covers.

We were hiding, wanting Grandma to think that we were sleep. I can remember that, but deception won't quite allow me to bring the details of this traumatic experience. It's quite interesting how the mind will deceive you.

I don't remember because maybe my mind doesn't want me to. Or maybe because after years of repressing memories, it seems like such a dark place to enter again. I mean if kissing a girl wasn't already bad enough, why did it have to be my cousin. And most importantly, why? What would make us even want to kiss? What would make us want to fondle? We were just kids in elementary school! Where did the idea become planted? Had she been thinking of kissing me all along? I certainly...just don't remember. I don't remember if it was I that even could have initiated it.

Was it something done to her? And maybe she thought it was ok for us? I'd never kissed a girl before, or even thought about it. So, why? Why on a regular day at Grandma's house did I experience such a perverted thing? Why was this seed planted in me? The scriptures say in James 1:13-15 that when after lust is conceived, it gives birth to sin. And then that sin, when it is full grown, dies. That day, my lust was conceived and gave birth to sexual perversion; that day was the beginning of my innocence dying.

The interesting part about history is this – you can't run from it! We, my cousin and I, have never spoken of it. In fact, it wasn't until the time when I knew that this book would be released that I **knew** I had to talk about it. It wasn't until I began to frantically fear that maybe my daughters and cousins, goddaughters and nieces would one day not only experience the same, but worse. I didn't understand why these conversations were shushed repeatedly. Most importantly, I needed to know how to kill the root of it all. Like I said, the interesting thing about history – you can never run from it!

Now what I experienced that day could be titled incest or could be considered something innocent that didn't matter. I would beg to differ that it was innocent seeing how years later, these same skeletons would surface – on the same side of the family.

Trust me, these are not things I "want" to talk about, especially in a book. These are things *necessary* to talk about. You know, when we see these instances in big time movies, we're entertained. We talk about what we would have done if we were in the character's shoes. We make judgements, probably unintentionally but still, they are judgments. We hate the characters that play such despicable roles, but we love the movies or sitcoms still. We engulf ourselves in the entertainment of the events. Well, though characters may someday tell this story on a television screen - I'm not going to dress this up with some fictional aspect. This is my story.

Just a few weeks before or after my fourteenth birthday, I laid in my bed one night watching a late-night movie with a male cousin. I'd lost my virginity only months earlier, but I wasn't promiscuous in the sense that I just *wanted* to have sex. I *actually* regretted it more than I knew and really didn't want to be "that" girl; because of this, I hadn't had sex more than twice at the moment this occurred. Yet, some kind of way that night, probably a weekend - there we laid (not in the same bed) watching a film that led to saturating our innocent eyes with sexually driven material.

(It's interesting to note also - the way I lost my virginity was through seeing a pornographic video given to me through my ex-boyfriend. I'll discuss this more later.) It, the movie, was low in volume because of course there was a conviction in us; knowing that we shouldn't be watching it. What came next, however unexpected it was, was still a line that we -*I'm sure*- both knew that shouldn't have been crossed.

But it happened, we had sex willingly with one another and the incest occurred. And because, remember, this is a part of my story I never wanted to tell or even wanted to be able to remember enough to tell - I don't. I don't remember every single moment. I don't. I can't. But I remember what we *spoke* before. I'm not sure why, but I do. He said something to the effect of, *"We ain't none but cousins."* I recall having what was a flirtatious conversation in a way, you know. After all, we are now under the influence of a very perverted nature. They were simple statements that held the weight of consent to our next moment.

I knew that it should have mattered that we were cousins, but I don't know why it didn't. What, at that moment, would cause two young people who knew such things were prohibited to reach those lines and go that far anyway? At any rate, I (as he did) gave verbal consent and it happened. Once again, my repressed memories forbid me to recall beginning to end. But I remember afterwards feeling dead, as he uttered the words, *"And you bet not be pregnant."*

It was just as it was in the Bible with Tamar and her half-brother, except without force. We'll talk about this later as well, but Amnon had a strong lust and raped his half-sister, Tamar. However, as soon as he slept with her, he hated her immediately. (2 Samuel 13)

I didn't hate him, but I felt such a weight, such a remorse. Day after day, trying to figure out how to cleanse myself of such a filth. I couldn't talk about it, and when I did to someone I trusted - I certainly didn't tell the version of the story as it actually happened.

How could that happen - me be truthful about such a thing? Yes, I knew better. No, I never even thought of him in that light again. Yes, I felt just as filthy and defiled as I should feel, year after year. But that does not answer the question: *How did that happen? How? And why?*

I would never have answers because as far as I was concerned, it never happened. Year after year, my cousin and I pretended to be solid. We never had a conversation about it, to this very day of me writing this book. But I am convinced that that moment changed his life just as much as it changed mine.

When I was 18, I committed to sexual purity and the Holy Spirit reminded me that it happened. Through fear, trembling and shame - I shared it during church, a very small church at that time. I was embraced; I felt relieved for that moment and once again, put it behind me. It didn't matter anymore right? All things are made new in Christ and every soul tie created before my new life with Christ was buried.

Right?

Well that's what I thought.

I had never even shared it with my family, not even the other cousins that I was close to. It was the deepest, darkest secret that I'd ever had and no one, *no one*, deserved to get that deep. It wasn't until over a decade later that the topic of inappropriate sex within family members came up. It was during a prayer meeting in which a few other close cousins and I had one day. As we conversed, I exposed in a very casual manner that I'd experienced incest within the family.

It was then like a light shone upon those darkest secrets and the skeletons began to talk. Though their experiences were not like mine, they were experiences still that affected them gravely. As we prayed, it angered us that it seemed like we became victims of a past that no one wanted to address. We recalled situations that we had vague memories of being discussed when we were little that may have hinted to the roots of what we saw in our own lives. I remember the three of us looking with blank stares at the conversation we'd just had.

What made me comfortable saying that at *that* point in my life? Why had the weight lifted? Why was I so free then when before, I would have rather died or lied out of that truth? I believe it was time to tell my truth, because no longer being afraid and ashamed of the truth was the breaking point to my freedom. It wasn't just my freedom, however, but the freedom of others.

My cousins breathed a sigh of relief, as if a burden had been lifted from their shoulders. But we all sat there with a reality: Each of us in our own way had experienced a form of sexual perversion that we didn't ask for - as if it was inherited. And that was not fair. We all had children, so a fear crept upon us at the very thought of our children's innocence being manipulated as ours was. So, then the question became: How do we keep this from happening to the next generation.

A skeleton: A framework of support, founding structure.

These sexual skeletons were the infrastructure to our past. No matter how we produced, or how much we didn't want to be like the previous generations - we were now as they were: because the basic structure to our sexual path had already been set.

It's like this - a seed planted in the ground is buried in the soil, but you don't ever see the seed, you only see the fruit of that seed. You see its stems, it's leaves, it's bark. You eventually see branches and, as long as that seed continues to be watered, it will grow. How do you kill a tree? You stop giving it what it needs to survive. Likewise, it is in the spirit.

Furthermore, you can identify a tree by its fruit - the types of leaves it produces, the type of bark it produces, even the type of climate it grows in. For example, a sycamore tree can't decide that it's going to produce pinecones or the balls of a sweetgum tree. Why? It isn't *genetically* designed to produce pines or sweet gum balls - it is designed to produce sycamore fruit. A sycamore tree produces fruit that are round and soft, whereas pine trees produces pinecones - which are full of aroma but prickly.

At the same time, a sweet gum tree produces a fruit that is round but prickly. See, it is by the characteristics *of* a tree one can immediately identify it. This is why the Word says you'll know them (false prophets) by their fruit. I also recall that Yeshua (Jesus) walked up to a tree that wasn't producing the fruit it should have produced, and he cursed it. (This is a powerful authority we'll also look at later.)

Do you see what I mean? I was taught to be a good little girl and save my virginity for my husband, as most my other girl cousins were, I'm sure. I wanted to do just that. I'm sure we all did. I often had convictions when I had sex or did anything in that nature that wasn't what I knew was right in my spirit. Yet there was something embedded in my (our) DNA that caused us to repeat the patterns from the people that told us not to be what we became. Why? More importantly, how?

What I came to understand was that our parents don't simply release natural DNA, but spiritual DNA as well. I came to furthermore understand that the Word was clear on sexual expectations; not just clear but adamant, and repetitive. Yahweh expected us to understand how important sex was and how important it was to be obedient to these restrictions upon us when it came to sex.

The restrictions were not to limit us for our bad, yet to protect us from what our Father knew would impact generations continually.

Zoë Dee

"Born in Sin, Shaped in Iniquity"

The scriptures are always the direction I turn to when I need an answer. I want to know what the Word says because it is the foundation of life to me. Therefore, I'm not going to expound on this subject through a mental, physical, or emotional aspect. We're simply going to the Word.

The Word says that we are born in sin and shaped in iniquity. Iniquity is the character of a sin - not necessarily the sin itself. I often say it is the difference between a person that lies once, is remorseful enough to not do it again and a person that is a liar, a person who lies habitually; between a person that cheats and a person that is a cheater. And it is the consequences of the sin and iniquities of our fathers that follow us.

Let's take a look at the story of Amnon and Tamar.

Amnon and Tamar are half brother and sister, whose father was David. David, though the apple of God's eye, fell into the sexual sin of adultery. What started with a lust in his eyes (think on it) ended with lies, adultery, and murder. Hmp, that sounds like a modern-day dramatic movie, right? Up until that point, David - a king- was successful in God's standards, you see.

However, the moment that this mighty man of God didn't protect His eye gates (think on it), he became enticed by Bathsheba's beauty and nudeness. Wait, that sounds like porn to me (think on it). Anyway, Bathsheba, the wife of Uriah, was taking a bath, when David saw her. Sin entered his heart through this lust, and he called for Bathsheba to be his. He slept with her. From that, she became pregnant. After David seeing that he couldn't cover his mess up using "his authority", he used "his authority" to kill the husband of Bathsheba - bringing mighty consequences upon his bloodline. The judgement released was that calamity would come upon not him, but his family!

How? First of all, the child he conceived was sick for days and then died. Then, two chapters down the line, we see Amnon take his sister Tamar and rape her. He lusted after her. The Bible says he burned with lust for her so that it made him sick! He devised wickedness in his own heart, driven by a lust he couldn't control! After he raped her, he hated her more than he ever even loved her and commanded she be removed from his presence. But the story doesn't end there.

Tamar had a brother, Absalom, also David's son. Absalom and Tamar were full brother and sister, and when he found out that his half-brother Amnon had raped his sister, what do you think happened? If you're thinking, "*Mane I woulda killed him on sight!*" then you're no different than Absalom, because that's exactly what he thought.

So, let's look at this.

David's lust, lies, adultery, and murder according to the Bible brought upon an even greater tragedy - a division between his own family, with the fruit of his own seed (natural and spiritual). Each child was a natural seed by the physical, genetic realm and by default they were affected by David's spiritual seeds of lust, lies, adultery and murder. Remember we said in the last chapter that a seed *only* produces fruit after its *own* kind. What did Tamar do to deserve to be raped? Nothing. She even tried to beg Amnon to let David marry her, warning him that what he was about to do would be completely shameful.

Amnon refused that and used "*his* authority" to rape her. Isn't it interesting that David used "*his* authority" to take Bathsheba, another man's husband? Do we see that both of these instances reflect a "rape?' Although Bathsheba didn't say no, it was the authority of his position as king that David used to take her. For Amnon, it was the authority of his natural strength. It had to have been a woman within David's bloodline otherwise it would not have been "fruit" of his spiritual seed, because once again, your fruit only produces from the seed that was originally planted or sown.

Therefore, Amnon became a rapist, just as his father. And Absalom became a murderer, just as his father. And Tamar became defiled, just as the child was that was conceived with David and Bathsheba was defiled. Think on this, every seed that you sow not only affects you but your children - this could be a great thing but could also be a horrible thing.

So, David lusted and committed adultery with Bathsheba, defiling the marriage bed of Uriah and then also killed Uriah however, when the judgement was released David said, "*I have sinned against the Lord.*" Ultimately, that's who our sins are against. Though we commit them in the natural, because we are a spirit and made in His image and likeness, anything outside of this image and likeness is against the Father. And see because we all are made in His image and likeness, what we do each other, we do to Him. What we do to Him, we do to each other.

Though he committed adultery with Bathsheba in the natural, he committed adultery against the Father and then defiled the holiness within Bathsheba. The result of any sin is death. James 1:13-15 puts it like this:

13 When tempted, no one should say, "God is tempting me." For God cannot be tempted by evil, nor does he tempt anyone; 14 but each person is tempted when they are dragged away by their own evil desire and enticed. 15 Then, after desire has conceived, it gives birth to sin; and sin, when it is full-grown, gives birth to death.

When we give into the temptation of our sinful nature by acting upon it, we produce sin. There is no sin that we can play with that will not produce a death, whether spiritual or physical. This is why we have to be careful with our decisions. Most importantly, we have to realize that we are sowing spiritual seeds that will produce fruit that not "may" affect our children but *will* affect our children.

Let's look at the scriptures again:

Exodus 34:7 tells us that the Lord will not leave the guilty unpunished! "...maintaining love to thousands, and forgiving wickedness, rebellion and sin. Yet he does not leave the guilty unpunished; he punishes the children and their children for the sin of the fathers to the third and fourth generation."

This is the power of our influence on the Earth! Did you know that even the Father uses the word "household" that He isn't referring to just a unit of a mother, father, sister, and brother? No, when God sees family, He sees generations! That's why our seeds are blessed, but it is also why they may fall at the hand of our wickedness! There are so many examples in the Bible when God saved *households*, i.e. entire families. We must understand the mind of God to understand how crucial it is to stay in His destiny for us! But here's something even more frightening. As if it's not bad enough that your sins can follow your children, great grandchildren, great-great grandchildren, and great-great-great grandchildren, - the consequences of sexual sins carry a longer term!

(Deu. 23:2 NIV) No one born of a forbidden marriage nor any of his descendants may enter the assembly of the LORD, even down to the tenth generation.

What makes one married to another? The act of engaging in sex. The Bible states that when a man and woman have sex, the two shall become one. Right? So, any forbidden sex by default brings the consequences of these sexual sins upon not just you, but your family line.

My Personal Testimony:

Before the fire of the Holy Spirit fell upon me September 2017, I had once again started playing with sexual sin. I was unmarried and having sex without covenant, writing sexual books, hosting a podcast sharing my perverted thoughts, *and* entertaining women sexually. The biggest thing for me was my lust for women. I had walked in and out of that lifestyle for many years. Although I committed to purity at 18, and I was cleansed - along the years as I rebelled against God, those desires came back and came back with a vengeance.

The day of my fire experience though, I begin to vomit a clear substance for several minutes. I believe that the Holy Spirit told me that it was the spirit of bisexuality. He told me exactly why I had battled it, what part of my bloodline it came from and what sin it was a result of! Then He said, *"You will not take that mess into your marriage."*

Yes, my mind was so reprobate that I knew that when I got married - either my husband and I both would have random but consensual sexual relationships with other women or I would have them by myself because *"Maybe that's just the way we're meant to be,"* as I told myself and others. So, as I write this book and share the defiling details of my past life, I tell it with full confidence that the Word is the only truth that is needed!

Though I had committed again to celibacy by the time I had my fire experience, my Father was making sure that I would not return to the grounds of that illegal sex. I share this experience in more detail in the title *#aCall2Purity*, so I won't go fully into the other areas of that testimony.

What I believe the Holy Spirit wants to make known to you at this moment is that there is a linkage to our family's sin and disobedience. Notice, David was given a choice, and he chose sin. David's sin was adultery, because Bathsheba was married. After all, he had many other wives and concubines; yet he desired what belonged to another man.

Selah.

We cannot escape the law of seed and harvest, sowing and reaping. It is written that we will reap what we sow, my dear brothers and sisters - it is not a theory. It is a fact that what we sow, we shall reap, and God will not be mocked.

You may feel that you don't have a choice in the matter and this point and accept what would seem like defeat. I have some good news, matter of fact, great news for you. See, though the laws of seed and harvest are in effect - there is also such as the law of grace, mercy, redemption, and love. Because of the blood of the lamb, our Savior Jesus Christ - we are free from the curses of our ancestors. We are in fact evidence of the curse being broken. We do not have to walk in the ways of bondage of our forefathers. But we do have to repent, repent for our forefathers, be cleansed, and make a choice who we will choose to serve.

Zoë Dee

Consensual

Whether you know it or not, we give permission to the enemy by what we *say*. See, the enemy is aware that he cannot go where he is not permitted or do anything that he is not permitted, otherwise he is out of jurisdiction. The enemy cannot do anything that God doesn't allow him to do. But...

He can do and enter into a place or person that gives him permission to. So, I'll share another example from my own life. As I said, before my fire experience - I had committed to sexual purity again; and not because I wanted to. I had an experience that woke me up to the dangers that I was playing with. Because I was already engaged in sexual perversion and writing sexually perverted material, I had given the enemy plenty of permission to guide my life.

Well, I recall this one show that I was used to watch and the lady was the mother of dragons. I was in love with this character and verbally spoke, *"If I could have any power or be any character - I would be her."* Of course, I spoke her name and etc. but for the sake of legal purposes I won't get into details. Anyway, *verbal consent,* right? I came in agreement with just a "character" on a "show." Or at least that's what we like to believe. No, I came into agreement with the *spirit* of that character! Anyway...

One night during sex, as we were in the act of having sex, I heard a voice in my mind say the name, *"Leviathan."* I say that I believe that it was my spirit because remember, I'm in the act of sex - my mind was only focused on what my body was feeling at that moment. Besides, I had never heard of that before. I didn't know who he was or why I was thinking about him at that moment. What happened next was truly a spiritual experience. My spirit or the Holy Spirit then said, *"Jesus is Lord. Jesus is Lord. Jesus is Lord."* I say my spirit because I understand that I am a spirit and my spirit can hear the voice of the Holy Spirit when He speaks to me. However, because I do not think that my spirit was as strong, I believe the Holy Spirit intervened. Either way, it wasn't something I ever thought with my own natural senses; that is the point.

Now, I never stopped my sex partner or removed him from inside of me. I never stopped my body from engaging in the orgasmic pleasure my flesh was enduring. But afterwards, I knew that there had been a divine intervention over my soul and spirit. I knew that I had been covered somehow again by my Father.

Right there, a spiritual battle had taken place. I had to wonder what it was, or who it was, should I say. So, as I do, I sought the scriptures. I found the mention of him in Job 41. God is speaking to Job and describing Leviathan as a horrific sea creature, who very much resembles what we would call a dragon. (How intriguing that the same "character" I loved was the mother of dragons.) This Leviathan is one of the strongest spiritual entities in the demonic realm. It is not just a demon; it has a higher rank. Remember Ephesians 6 says we wrestle not against flesh and blood but against principalities and powers.

As I did my study inside and outside of the Bible, I found that this demonic entity is often on assignment to ministries. Other characteristics of this principality are control, deception, and anxiety. It is often times in operation when you see a person trying to read their Bible or stay awake in church. They are in spiritual opposition because the assignment of this principality is to stunt spiritual growth.

Had the enemy had his way that night, I would not be writing this book and would probably be dead by now. I'm not exaggerating - I was given a choice the day of my fire experience. I could complete the mandate that was on my life or come home (die) early. It all goes back to consent. We have, as Joshua said (24:14-15), a choice to make. We must choose who we will serve! So, let's address this:

My Leviathan experience came as a consent with my mouth and then my actions. Notice, I engaged in sex without covenant, which opened me up spiritually to that attack - because *sex is spiritual.* But first it started with what I was watching. When I experienced incest, once again I was watching a perverted show, then I spoke consent and the act happened. When I wanted to know what sex was, I was given a porn tape and watched it, then consented to it.

Remember the enemy gets permission to move in your life by what you agree with him on. We have to take responsibility for what the devil does in our lives. We need to protect our ears, eyes, and the words we speak. We cannot watch *anything* we want to because writers, producers, and the powers that be are not always under the influence of God the Father, Yahweh, when they produce these visuals. Trust me, it's more of an agenda than you think. I sit and wonder why this particular show with the "mother of dragons" was so popular.

Not only that, in this same show, there was much sexual immorality, even incest. See? Again, we take things so lightly - being blinded by what's really right in our face! Most of the problems that we face today do begin with our forefathers and that is the purpose of this book. But let us be even more real. Many things God has shown us, and even freed us from and we give consent to devil and go right back into those things, making our consequences even worse. We watch anything we want to watch. We listen to anything and everything we want to listen to. Even worse, we allow our natural seeds to do the same.

We have to understand that we are spirits and everything that we put into our natural gates will either feed or starve our spirits. If our spirit is starved, our flesh will devour us with the fleshly desires – which produces sin and death. See the reason I had to make the decision to let God purify my life was because the books that I was writing was under the spirit of Balaam – a sexual perverted spirit. The enemy took what should have been my greatest deliverance and tried to use it to influence people into more sexual defilement. I knew that I was wrong. My previous books glorified the enemy's work over and over again and because of that, I was in an extremely dangerous place claiming to be a believer of Yahweh doing so.

The result? I was given a choice: I could keep writing those books, blogs, hosting those podcasts and tours. I could exploit myself using sex and be another "*Gone too soon sweet young lady.*" Isn't this what we see in our culture - our stars rise promoting themselves through sex? Why? Let me give you a hint

- pagan worship included sexual rituals. Don't believe me? Read your Bible. Start with Leviticus 18. Yes, put this book down and go read the chapter!

Now, let's read this Numbers 25: 1 - 8

And Israel abode in Shittim, and the people began to commit whoredom with the daughters of Moab.

> ***PAUSE: The daughter of Moab was Lot's children; who if you don't remember, were children born of incest. Lot's daughters slept with him while he was drunk. Ok... (Genesis 19:30-38)***

2 And they called the people unto the sacrifices of their gods: and the people did eat and bowed down to their gods.

3 And Israel joined himself unto Baal-peor: and the anger of the Lord was kindled against Israel.

4 And the Lord said unto Moses, "Take all the heads of the people, and hang them up before the Lord against the sun, that the fierce anger of the Lord may be turned away from Israel.

> ***PAUSE: If God has no problem with our sexual "freedom", why did He immediately want these people who were having sex with the Moabites to die?? He didn't say kill them, He basically said, "OFF WITH THEIR HEADS!" Think on that the next time you think it's your body and you can sleep with who you want to. Ok...***

5 And Moses said unto the judges of Israel, slay ye everyone his men that were joined unto Baal-peor.

6 And, behold, one of the children of Israel came and brought unto his brethren a Midianitish woman in the sight of Moses, and in the sight of all the congregation of the children of Israel, who were weeping before the door of the tabernacle of the congregation.

> *Do you see what is happening? The boldness of this man. He brought the woman right in front of everyone and took her into the tent. Everyone knew what was about to happen!*

7 And when Phinehas, the son of Eleazar, the son of Aaron the priest, saw it, he rose up from among the congregation, and took a javelin in his hand;

8 And he went after the man of Israel into the tent, and thrust both of them through, the man of Israel, and the woman through her belly. So the plague was stayed from the children of Israel.

> *Yes, Phinehas got up and killed both for the sin that they brought in the presence of God's people! First of all, let's not pretend as if it was fine and that it was his business to do what he wanted to do. Why not? Let's read the next verse.*

9 And those that died in the plague were twenty and four thousand.

> *That sin that was consensual caused death upon 24,000 people. Do you still believe it's "just sex" and that you own your body and have the freedom to connect it to whomever you choose?*

No, we have to understand that the sexual sins of our fathers and forefathers are indeed held to a judgement and that judgement brings consequences. God did not change His mind.

He still expects us to be clean. He still expects us to be holy. I end this chapter with my personal testimony:

After the last sexual experience I had, I didn't desire sex anymore - at least not in that way. I became obedient to God, living pure and honoring His word through my writing. Four hundred days later, God blessed me to come into my covenant marriage – one He had prophesied months earlier. Not only that, but the Holy Spirit also made sure that I knew that I had been sexually clean for four hundred days. I personally believed that this was intentional.

If you think of the numbers 4, 40, and 400 - each are significant in a new dispensation of power. Four represents a generation; forty represents testing, trial (ex. Jesus fasted that many days before he was tempted and passed His test); 400 represents bondage but perfected timing. The children of Israel were in bondage 400 years and then walked in their freedom. We (the children of Israel) were again promised 400 years of slavery in the Bible.

The four hundred days represented not just a symbolism of great strength but a perfecting time that my obedience would break the curses not just from my life but the next generations. I was chosen and destined to be a leader and show forth the deliverance of God in the area of sexual immorality. The enemy knew that and used everything he could to break me early and pervert me to where I never thought I would be clean enough to come back to my Father. However, my Father, being the most gracious God that He is - reversed that death and called me into life. He breathed on me His fire. He placed His Words in my mouth, and His heart in my heart.

He set me on fire - to warn and gracefully bring back those too that are lost; and that is the final purpose of this book. To conclude, let us pray:

Father in the name of Jesus we come thanking you for who you are and repenting of everything that we have done to displease you – especially in the area of sexual sin. Father we repent of the sins of our forefathers and ourselves. We declare that the blood of Jesus has made us free from the curses of sin and death, therefore we invoke our spiritual authority and declare freedom from all sexual sins, inherited and consensual. Jesus purge us, cleanse us and set us on fire to live sexually pure for you. Heal us of any wounds caused by the past and restore our hearts to a place of perfection and love. We declare that you are Lord over our lives, and over our bodies. In Jesus' name, Amen.

Scriptural References:

Matthew 7:15-20

Mark 11:12-25

Psalm 51:5

Genesis 1:27

2 Samuel Chapters 11 - 13.

Matthew 2:24

Galatians 6:7

Zoë Dee

About the Author

A product of statutory rape and a by-product of adultery, Zoë Dee passionately travels state-wide sharing her story and teaching young and old how to escape the strongholds and oppression related to premarital sex and adultery by the power of God. She is an educator, entrepreneur, and international known author. Zoë has authored nine titles as including the compelling writings *#aCall2Purity*, *The Strange Woman*, *Sexually Wise*, and *40 Day to Freedom* Devotional Journal.

After nine years of teaching, Zoë left the public classroom to pursue full time entrepreneurship as a speaker, publisher, and life coach. In doing so, she has become a highly respected and desired speaker, as she pours life into every ear that listens. Though no longer in the traditional classroom, she offers her teaching gift to the church, allowing the gift to be manifested teaching young people the Word of God.

After an immensely powerful encounter with the Father, she has committed her life to motivate and dare her audience to answer the call to purity. In addition to this – she is a wife, mother, exhortation life coach, and manager multiple family owned businesses.

.

Current Titles by Author

- #aCall2Purity
- **Sexually Wise**
- **Sexual Skeletons**
- **40 Days to Freedom**
- **War Wounds** *(Prayer book for teachers)*
- **Confessions for Wives** *(Prayer book for wives)*

Zoë also blogs at www.zoedeespeaks.com

Upcoming Titles by Author

- **The Strange Woman (November 2020)**
- **Circumcise My Heart (2021)**

Zoë is available for guest speaking engagements as well as her #aCall2Purity keynote message/course.

For more information on booking please contact:

booking@zoedeespeaks.com or

witnesslegend.com/zoedeespeaks

Connect with Zoë on social platforms on

Facebook, Instagram, Twitter, and YouTube

@ "Zoë Dee Speaks."

www.ingramcontent.com/pod-product-compliance
Lightning Source LLC
Chambersburg PA
CBHW071743150426
43191CB00010B/1676